Trading with the Trendlines
The Power of Divergence

DAVID CARLI

Trading foreign exchange on margin carries a high level of risk, and may not be suitable for all investors. The high degree of leverage can work against you as well as for you. Before deciding to invest in foreign exchange, you should carefully consider your investment objectives, level of experience, and risk appetite. No information or opinion contained in this book should be taken as a solicitation or offer to buy or sell any currency, or other financial instruments or services. Past performance is no indication or guarantee of future performance.

Copyright © Fifth edition April 2020 by David Carli.

All rights reserved. This book or any portion thereof may not be reproduced or used in any manner whatsoever without the express written permission of the publisher except for the use of brief quotations in a book review.

This cover has been designed using images from Freepik.com.

All images in the book are charts taken from the TradingView.com website. As stated in point 4 of their Privacy (https://www.tradingview.com/policies/) I am authorised to use these charts. So, for Amazon and others, this book does not break any laws.

First Printing: 2016

ISBN: 9798645292959

Website: www.tradingwithdavid.com
E-mail: info@tradingwithdavid.com

EDITED

Caroline Winter
carolinewinter4@hotmail.com

Contents

Introduction – About the Author   1

Introduction – About TradingView   2

Introduction – Preface   3

Chapter 1 – Commodity Channel Index   12

Chapter 2 – The Strategy   15

Chapter 3 – Money Managements   17

Chapter 4 – Final Comments   21

Appendix A – Web Resources   24

About the Author
INTRODUCTION

My journey in the investment and trading world started shortly after I graduated from the University of Pisa, Italy. I then travelled to New York City USA., where I attended exclusive courses by Steve Nison who introduced the western world to the art of the Japanese candlestick as a tool for analysing market trends and investment decisions.

I have been working as a full-time trader and an independent financial analyst since 2007 hence I established Trading with David as a niche investment service with the primary focus on FX markets and commodities. During that time, I collaborated with reputable financial trading services and investment magazines. And from 2012 -2013 I worked as a hedge fund manager for an Italian Bank boutique. In 2018, I began providing market analysis and trading ideas for a major European commodity investment company up to this date.

I published several trading and investment books to pass on my knowledge and expertise on how to analyse the financial market correctly and have the odds on your side to become a profitable trader. My approach is based on low-risk investment strategies across all markets to achieve a balanced asset allocation through diversification and risk management.

I have several other books for those who wish to learn more about certain aspects of trading such as Forex, Commodities Spread Trading, and Options so you can see how I approach other markets. Through educational channels, I coach independent investors on my personal trading strategies and how to apply them in different market conditions.

You can find out more about my educational library on https://tradingwithdavid.com to develop an extraordinary edge to your trading and investments plan with a deep understanding of the macro environment, along with advanced analysis and risk management they are designed to build or improve your trading skills.

About TradingView
INTRODUCTION

My favourite trading platform is TradingView. While I have used many other platforms in the past, I have found this innovative platform has all tools and versatility that once were only reserved for investment firms' players. The popularity of this platform among active traders ranging from institutional traders, financial software companies, and retail traders is a testament to its user-friendly interface.

Created by MultiCharts as a browsing web-based charting platform. It offers a multitude of features that allow market enthusiasts to connect and collaborate via a chat window, sharing ideas and exchange opinions in real-time - this is particularly useful for those who wish to follow a certain style of trading by following specific members without the need to subscribe to their chat room at an extra cost.

Another feature that is extremely important for active traders is the ease of writing scripts. The programming language that TradingView designed is called Pine Script, it's lightweight yet powerful which lets anyone develop their own proprietary indicators and strategies to be published on the community hub.

The platform has one of the largest social networks driven by traders and investors who contribute trading ideas for the public to interact with and learn from – a place where top analysis and valuable content are presented daily by professional traders globally. With over 100 ready-to-use indicators, and over 5000 scripts commonly used for researching and backtesting. TradingView lets you discover a new world of trading and showcase your talent by being a part of a dynamic and robust community of traders.

And if speed of trade execution is your priority, TradingView allows you to integrate your account directly with your brokerage account.

Personalization is truly the greatest aspect of this platform; you could build spreads and compare two or more charts with ease. Every single instrument can be customised, and every detail can be modified. It has been my preferred charting platform for all the reasons mentioned above and more - you will be able to follow my new trading ideas and the articles that I regularly publish on TradingView to expand your knowledge and improve your trading.

Preface
Introduction

"*The Power of Divergence*" is the second volume of the series "Trading with the Trendlines." The book explains a strategy that is applicable in every market (forex, equities, commodity...), and which is a combination of divergence, trendlines and a bit of Fibonacci; it is a simple strategy that seeks to exploit the reversal of a market.

What you will read in the book is the correct way to use divergences, in particular, the one between the price and Commodity Channel Index (CCI). Every aspect is well explained, including proper position sizing, through many examples.

Identifying the target profit and stop-loss of this strategy is both easy and clear. Not only this. Depending on your account, I will also explain to you the correct position sizing, to enable you to have proper money management.

If you are a beginner, do not worry; the first two chapters will provide you with adequate knowledge for understanding the strategy and using it correctly.

Do not be tricked by the fact that this book is widely distributed at printing price. The strategy, if you use it correctly and with the appropriate money management for your account, will give you a high percentage of profitable trades.

However, combining this strategy with fundamental analysis is recommended, as is opening a position only if both give the same signal.

You can read my free analyses about this and other strategies on **TradingView** (https://www.tradingview.com/u/TradingwDavid). All you have to do is sign up (as I said, this is free) and follow me.

For any question, do not hesitate to contact me at the e-mail address info@tradingwithdavid.com, it will be my pleasure to answer all of you. Also, visit my website https://tradingwithdavid.com, where you will find free articles, analyses, and books.

Commodity Channel Index

CHAPTER 1

The Commodity Channel Index (CCI) is an indicator created and developed by Donald Lambert specifically for the study of commodities, but that was soon after adopted for the analysis of other financial markets as well.

The function of the CCI is to measure the change in prices compared to their historical-statistical average to identify the highs and lows of market cycles. The basic principle is simple and logical: to identify and highlight the anomalies and the euphoric-depressive excesses that have historically occurred in the financial markets.

Figure 1 - Walt Disney, Commodity Channel Index (TradingView.com)

High values in the Commodity Channel Index mean there is a price trend that is too high in comparison to its historical average. Likewise, too low values indicate unusually depressed prices. The logic, therefore, is to identify an excess in prices and wait for a signal warning that the market is realigning its values to the real ones.

Generally, the area of oscillation of the indicator varies between the values of -150 and 150. Extreme zones are considered levels of overbought (CCI> 100) and oversold (CCI <100).

You can see the Commodity Channel Index applied to the Walt Disney chart in figure 1 above.

I will not talk about the signals that the Commodity Channel Index generates but how I use the indicator within the strategy that I am going to explain in the next chapter.

Also because, if the traditional use of indicators and oscillators explained in all the books and websites concerning technical analysis were profitable, there would not be so many traders that blow their accounts every month.

What I do is look for divergences that form in the extreme zones of the indicator, trying to anticipate a trend inversion.

But what is divergence?

Divergence occurs when the price of an underlying asset is moving in the opposite direction to a technical indicator (for example there may be a divergence between price and volume, or between price and indicator).

In this case:

When price makes a lower low, but the CCI makes a higher low, what you have on the chart is a **bullish divergence**, as shown in figure 2.

Figure 2 – Bullish divergence price and CCI

Conversely, when price makes a higher high, but the CCI makes a lower high, you have a **bearish divergence**, as you can see in figure 3.

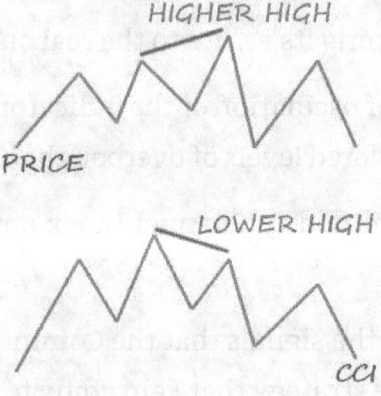

Figure 3 – Bearish divergence CCI and price

You can see a practical example of divergences in the Nvidia chart in figure 4.

Figure 4 - Nvidia, divergences (TradingView.com)

The combination of the CCI divergences, trendlines and a little bit of Fibonacci make up the strategy I am now going to explain in the following chapter.

THE STRATEGY

CHAPTER 2

A divergence often anticipates a trend inversion or the slowdown of a violent directional phase. Divergences may occur between different instruments, such as price, volume, indicators, etc. As you saw in the previous chapter, I use the Commodity Channel Index (CCI), as it is an excellent aid in finding "anomalous" situations within price trends. Moreover, using the more "extreme" overbought/oversold thresholds (+150/-150) of the Commodity Channel Index enables you to filter many false signals.

Thus, the Commodity Channel Index is far better than other indicators /oscillators because it provides an indication of bullish and bearish divergences, which are all the more valid if they occur in the excess zones (overbought/oversold) of the CCI (ideal range +150/-150).

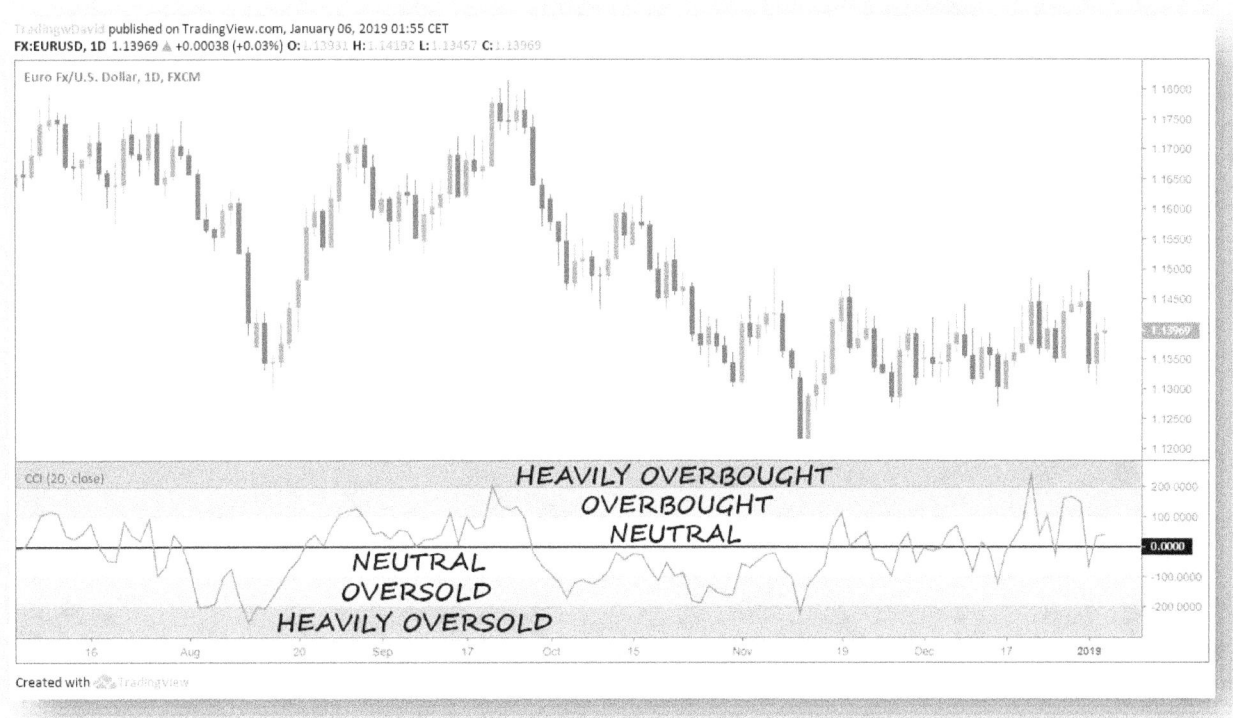

Figure 5 - Eur-Usd, CCI zones (TradingView.com)

Before I start explaining the strategy, I would first like to show you a chart from the Commodity Channel Index, because it visually summarises its meaning, and also offers some clarity. In figure 5 above, you can see the Eur-Usd daily chart. The different indicator zones have different colours.

Let's see now, in detail, the conditions under which a divergence should be formed. There are three simple rules to my strategy.

1. In a bullish divergence, the CCI should make the higher low in the oversold area below -150. In a bearish one, the indicator should draw the lower high in the overbought area above 150.

2. In a bullish divergence, the CCI should not rise above zero. In a bearish one, the indicator should not decrease below zero.

3. The second peak of the price should have a Fibonacci extension of 1.13, 1.272, 1.414, or 1.618. Over 1.618 the pattern is cancelled.

However, these rules are not strict, and some small exceptions can be granted. But let me show them to you in practice, by using some examples.

The **<u>first rule</u>** establishes the zone of the Commodity Channel Index in which the divergence should be formed: below -150 (bullish divergence), and above 150 (bearish divergence). Let me show you this concept in practice, using two examples.

Figure 6 - JD.COM, bullish divergence (TradingView.com)

Above, in figure 6, you can see a bullish divergence with the JD.COM daily chart, while in figure 7, the Eur-Nzd daily chart shows a bearish divergence. Both would have given a good profit.

Figure 7 - Eur-Nzd, bearish divergence (TradingView.com)

The ideal situation is when a divergence forms in the oversold (bullish) or overbought (bearish) areas. However, you can also accept an exception to this. The completion of the divergence (the second high or low) can take place slightly outside the areas mentioned above like it is happened in the Eur-Nzd example above.

The **second rule** states that in divergence, the Commodity Channel Index shall not go beyond zero, as shown below in figure 8 with Eur-Chf the chart.

As you can see from the chart above, the CCI never rises above zero during the divergence.

Even with this rule, you can accept an exception. You can tolerate a minimum overrunning of the zero. The important things are that it does not have to be deep, and it needs to take place only for a very short period of time. You can see an example in figure 9, again with Eur-Nzd daily chart.

Figure 8 - Usd-Chf, bullish divergence (TradingView.com)

Figure 9 - Eur-Nzd, bearish divergence (TradingView.com)

Finally, the **third rule**. Well, for sure, it is easier to explain with an example than with words, so take a look at the Usd-Cad daily chart (figure 10).

Figure 10 - Usd-Cad, bearish divergence (TradingView.com)

You have to calculate the Fibonacci extension of the last retracement, in the example above AB. The final peak should have an extension from 1.13 to 1.618 (this means: 1.130, 1.272, 1.414, or 1.618) of AB. Over 1.618 the pattern is cancelled. It is not complicated; every platform has the function for drawing Fibonacci retracements/extensions. With a bit of practice, everything about this strategy will become familiar to you.

Let us now turn to look at when you should open a trade, and how to calculate the stop-loss and target. The mere divergence is not in itself a valid signal to open a trade. It may also be possible that the divergence continues in the next days/weeks, and the price may touch new lows/highs. Therefore, there is a need for something that generates a stronger signal.

Below, you can see an example with the Eur-Nzd chart (figure 11). All you have to do is draw the trendline resistance (in a bullish divergence) or support (in the bearish one). The trendline breakout will give you the signal to open the trade.

The blue arrow indicates the candle that breaks the Eur-Nzd dynamic support and gives you the sell signal. There are more or less aggressive Strategies you can use to decide the trade entry. The more aggressive method is to open the position when the price crosses the trendline. In this way, you can be sure you will be inside the trade, but it also means risking being the victim of a false breakout.

Figure 11 - Eur-Nzd, bearish divergence (TradingView.com)

Figure 12 - Eur-Chf, bearish divergence (TradingView.com)

A less aggressive strategy is to wait for a close of the price beyond the trendline before opening a trade. The entry price will be worse, it will be lower than the more aggressive strategy seen above, but in this way, at least some fakeouts will be avoided.

The breakout of the trendline resistance-support grants you a significant signal because, once a divergence forms, there is no guarantee that the Price will rebound/reverse its trend, as it can continue to move as it did until then.

Look at the Eur-Chf daily chart above in figure 12. divergence and a short retracement, the price continued to rise. However, it did not break the trendline support and therefore did not generate any signals.

Even before clicking on "buy" or "sell" on the platform, you have to decide where to place the stop-loss and the target price.

The stop-loss is the easiest to determine and should be placed 15-20 pips/ticks below the last low (in a bullish divergence) or above the last high (in a bearish one) hit by the price. In the example from the Aud-Cad daily chart in figure 13, you can see it placed 15-20 pips below the last low of the currency pair.

Figure 13 - Aud-Cad, stop-loss (TradingView.com)

However, the stop-loss depends on the time-frame used. In a trade on a daily chart, it is correct to place a stop-loss 15-20 pips as mentioned above. In a 15-minute chart it would be too far away. Similarly, if you open a trade after a signal on a weekly chart, most likely 15-20 pips is too short a distance.

Therefore, you have to evaluate the stop-loss according to the time-frame used. Giving a general rule is wrong.

As regards the target, I still use Fibonacci. A 127.2% extension of the movement started with the last retracement of the price gives me the first target, where I close half the position and move the stop at break-even. A 161.8% extension identifies the second and last target.

You can examine how to calculate the correct Fibonacci extensions in more detail in figure 14 with the Eur-Nzd daily chart.

Figure 14 - Eur-Nzd, targets (TradingView.com)

So, at 1.68741 (127.2%) you close half the position, and at 1.67598 (161.8%) the other half (obviously, you can round the values up or down).

I have explained the rules for trading with divergences. Rules that serve to eliminate most false signals, although, with experience, you will find others. For example, it is not easy to open short trades following a bearish divergence on US equities.

Now, to complete this chapter, let's look at a series of other examples.

A bearish divergence on Eur-Nzd chart in figure 15 (already seen).

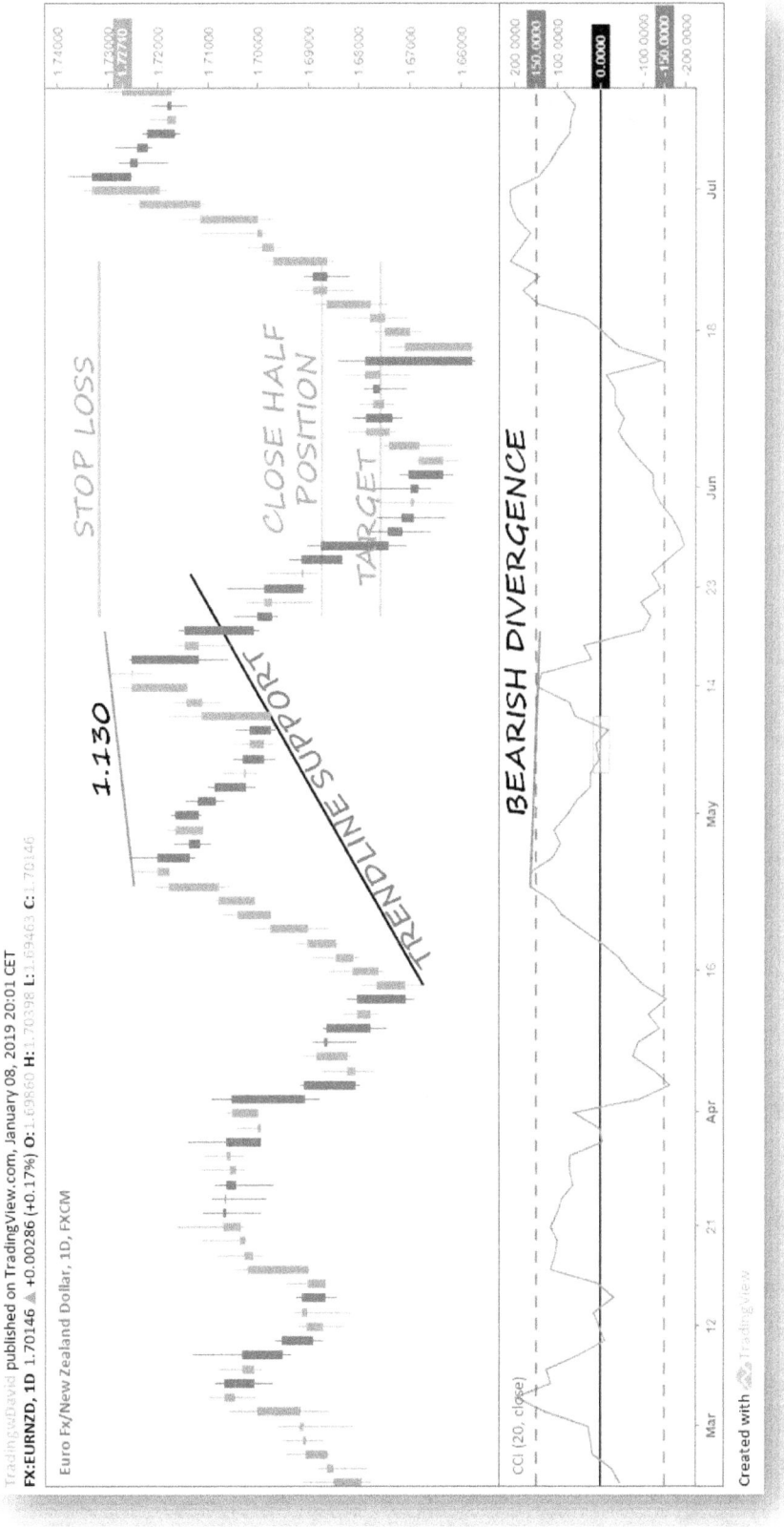

Figure 15 - Eur-Nzd, bearish divergence (TradingView.com)

A bearish divergence on the Apple chart in figure 16.

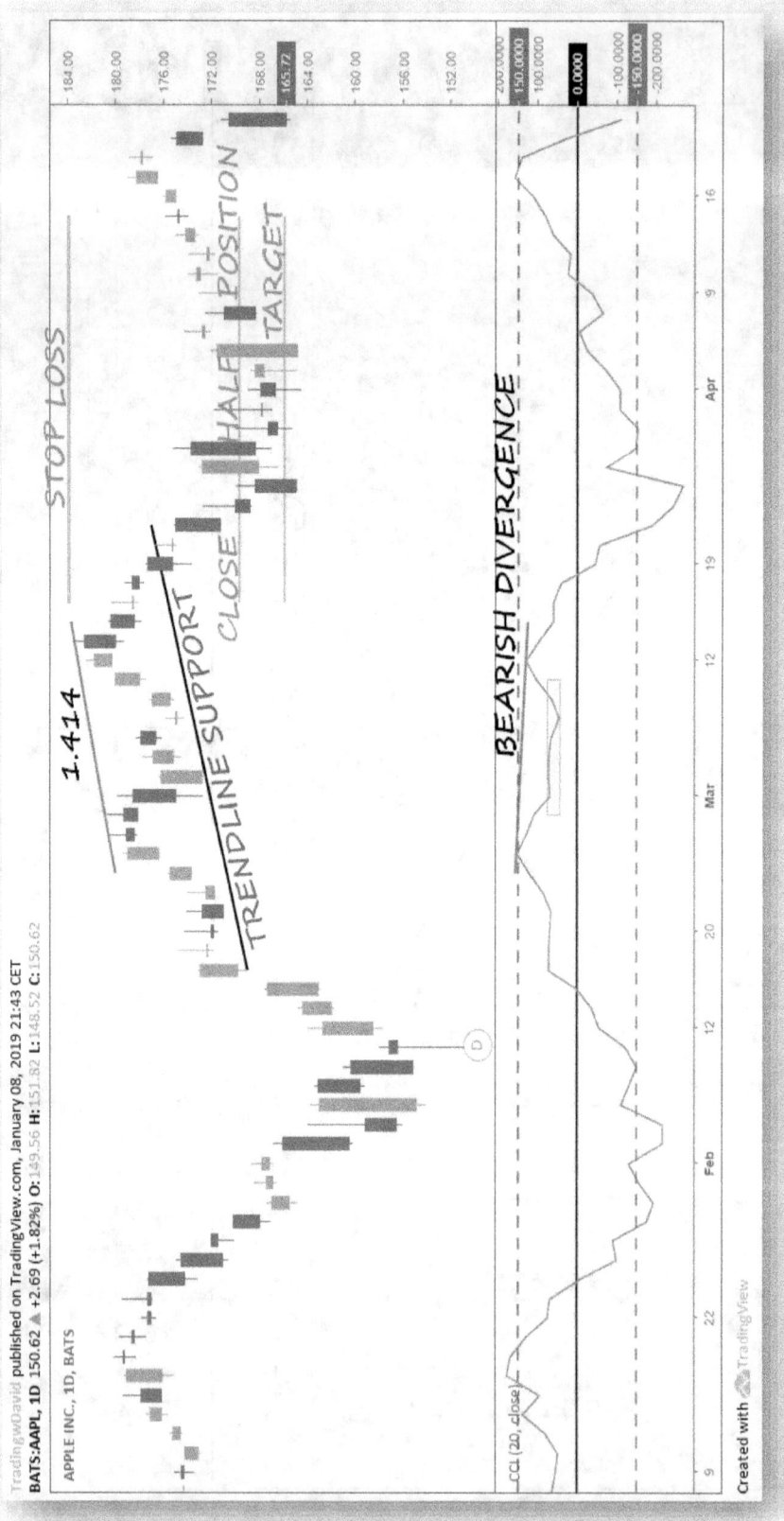

Figure 16 - Apple, bearish divergence (TradingView.com)

A bullish divergence on Usd-Chf chart in figure 17.

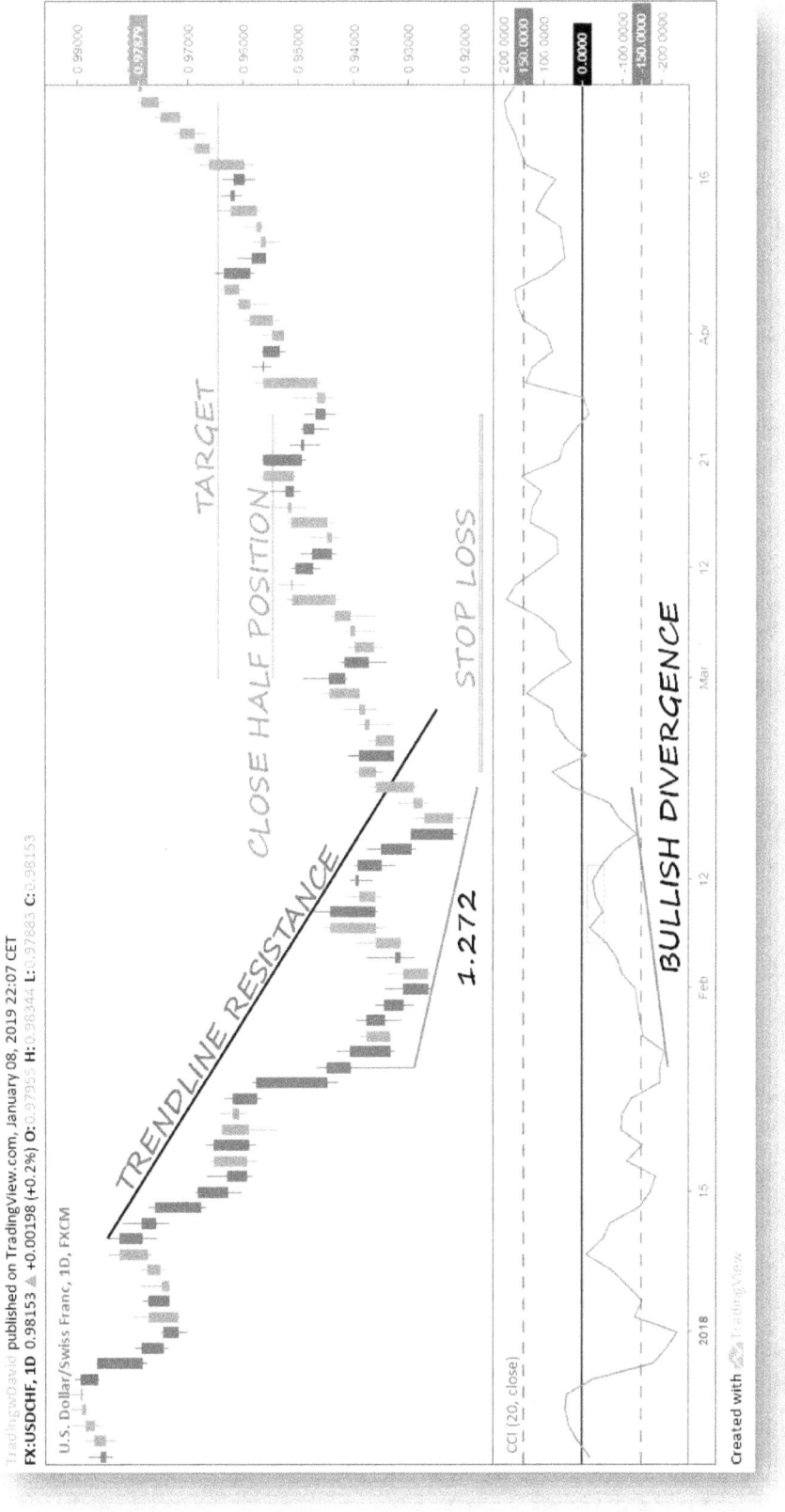

Figure 17 - Usd-Chf, bullish divergence (TradingView.com)

A bearish divergence on the gold chart in figure 18.

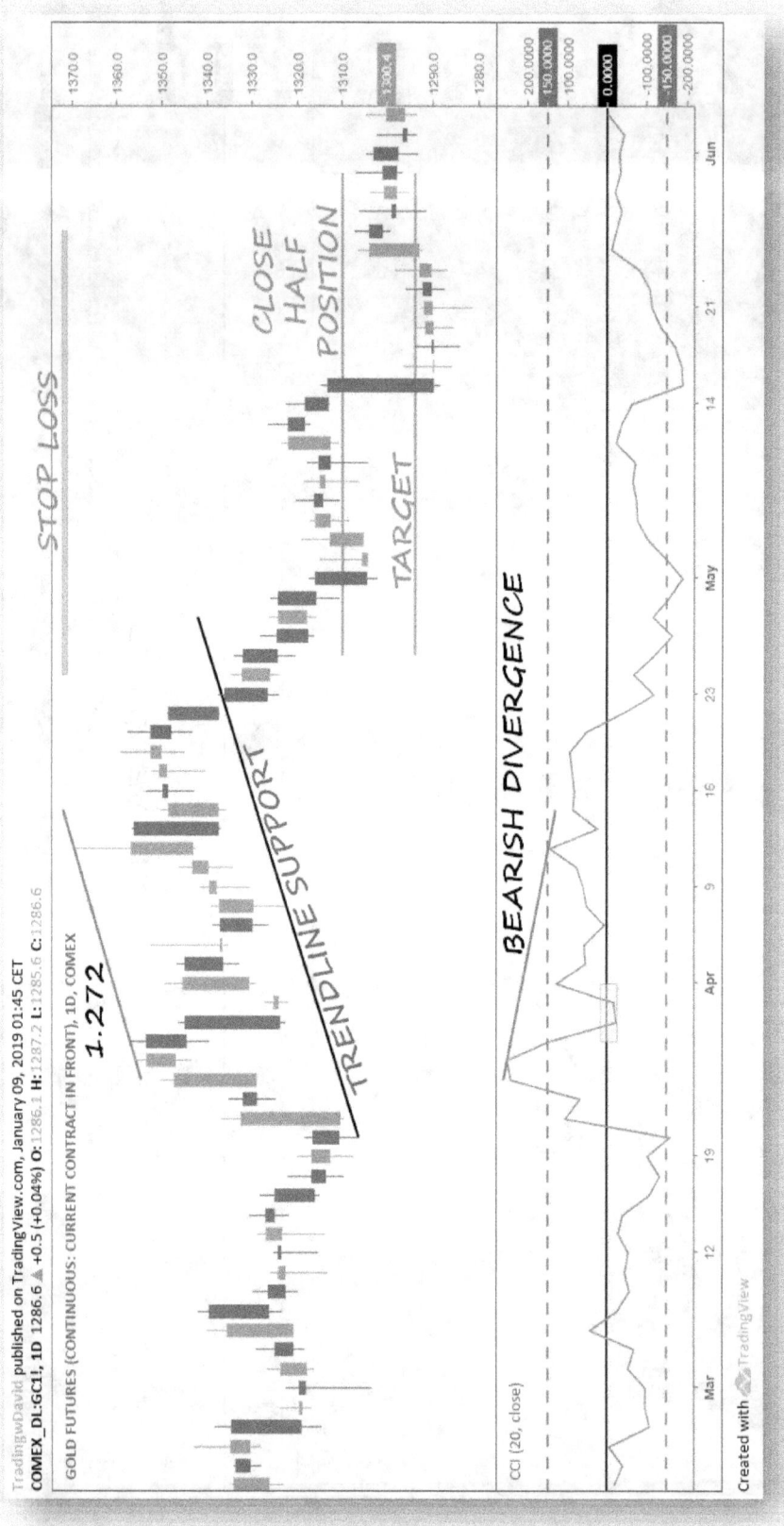

Figure 18 - Gold, bearish divergence (TradingView.com)

A bearish divergence on Gbp-Usd chart in figure 19.

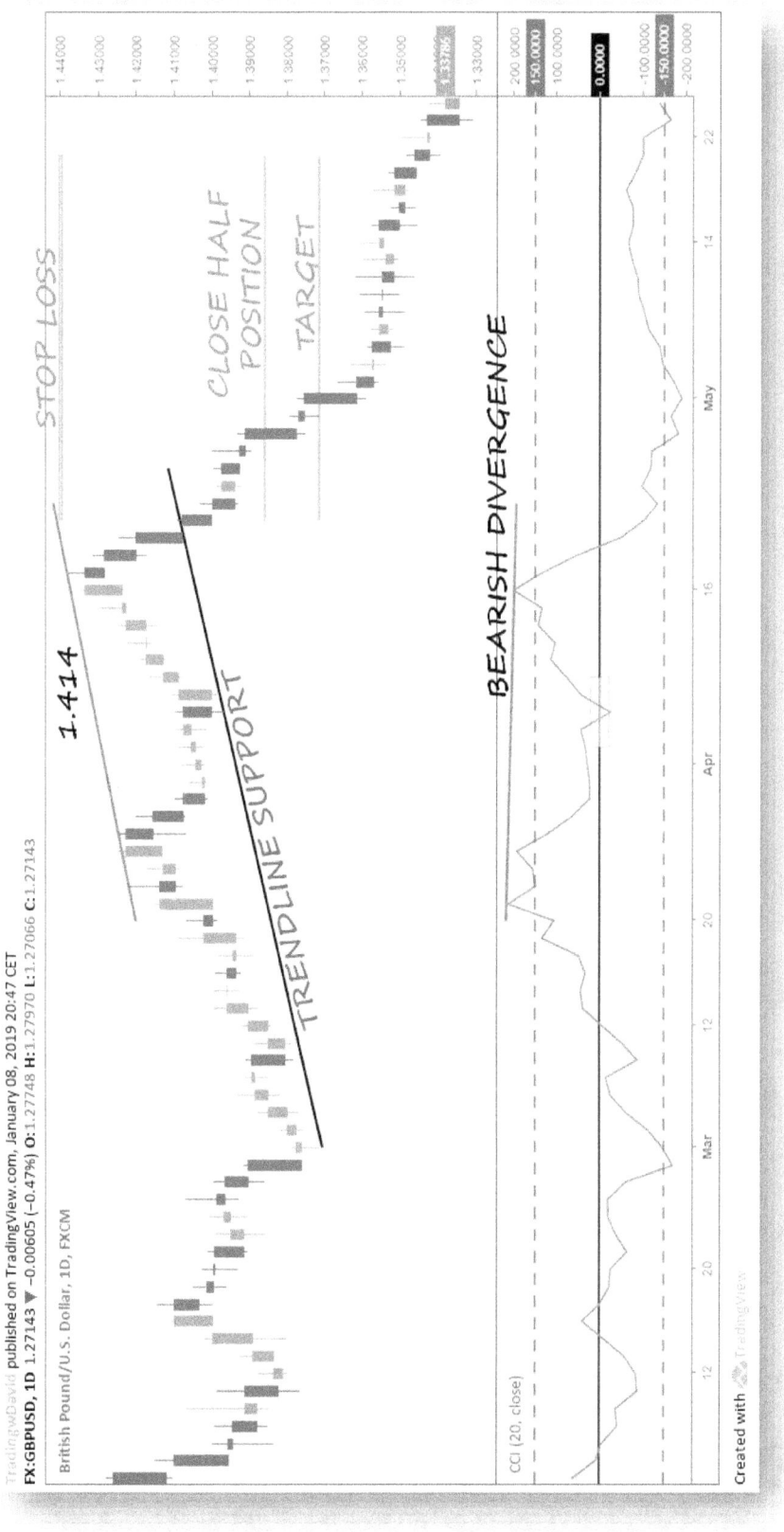

Figure 19 - Gbp-Usd, bearish divergence (TradingView.com)

A bullish divergence on Berkshire Hathaway chart in figure 20.

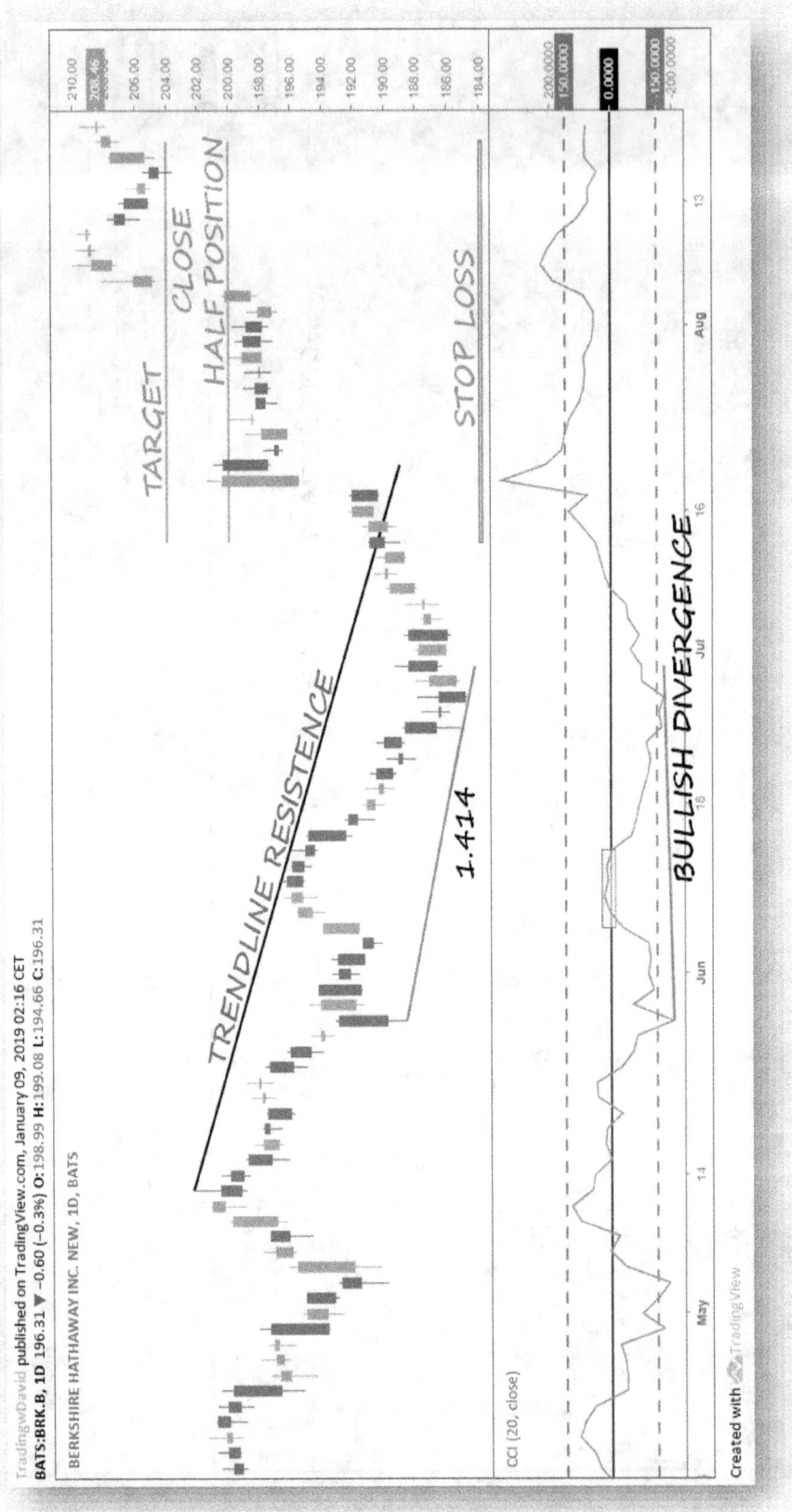

Figure 20 - Berkshire Hathaway, bearish divergence (TradingView.com)

A bearish divergence on Usd-Cad chart in figure 21.

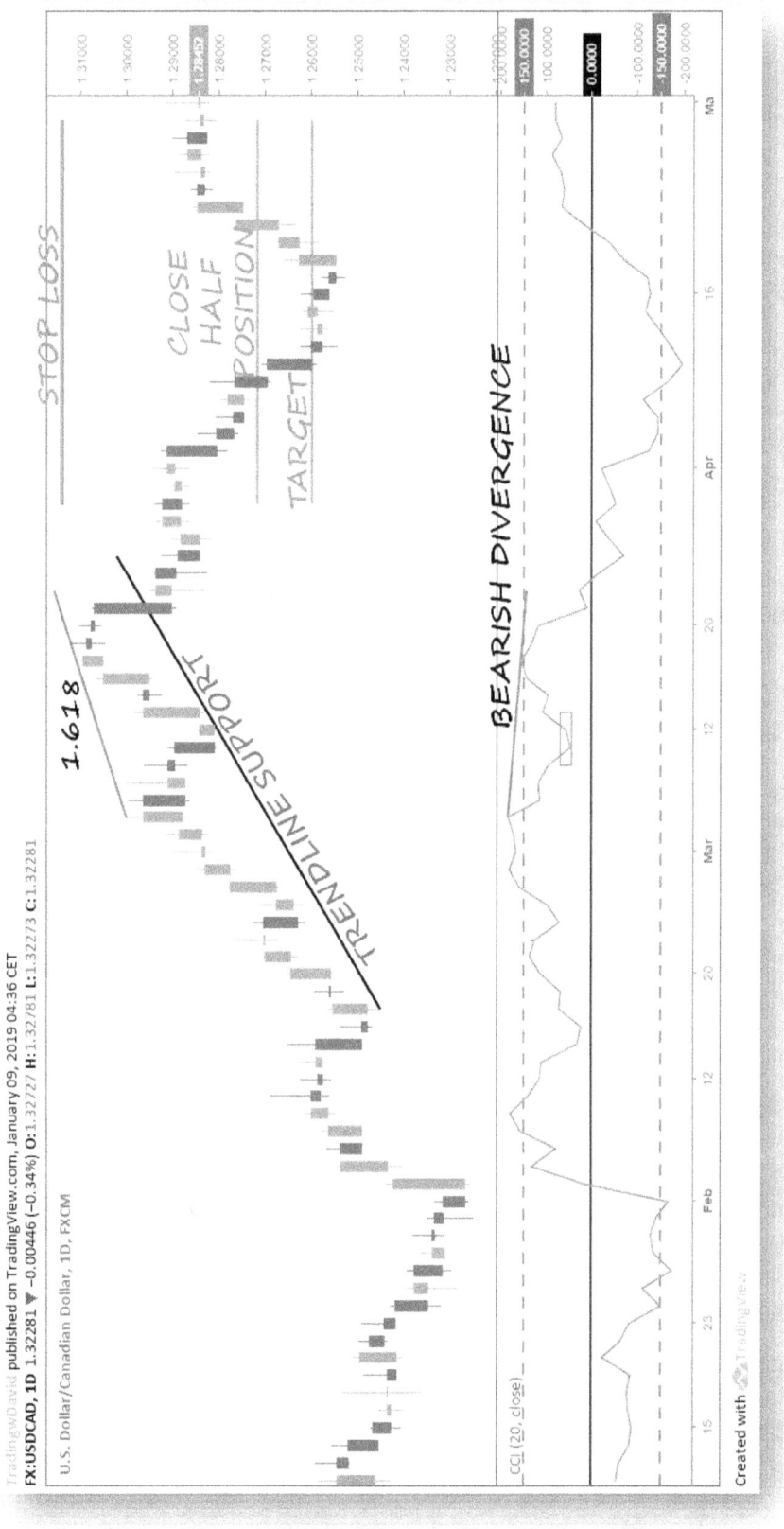

Figure 21 - Usd-Cad, bearish divergence (TradingView.com)

A bearish divergence on the Nasdaq 100 futures chart in figure 22.

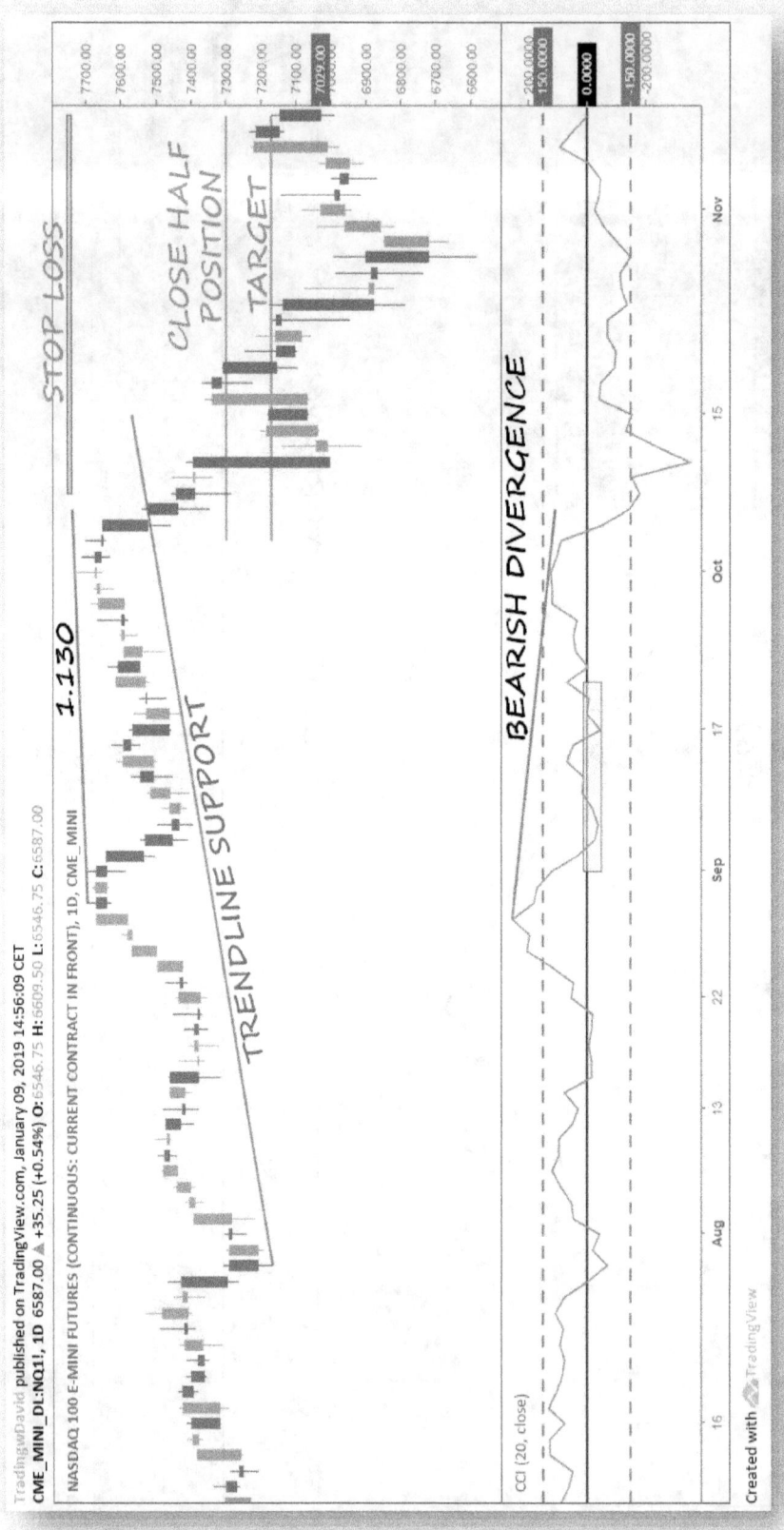

Figure 22 - Nasdaq 100 futures, bearish divergence (TradingView.com)

A bullish divergence on BTC-Usd chart in figure 23.

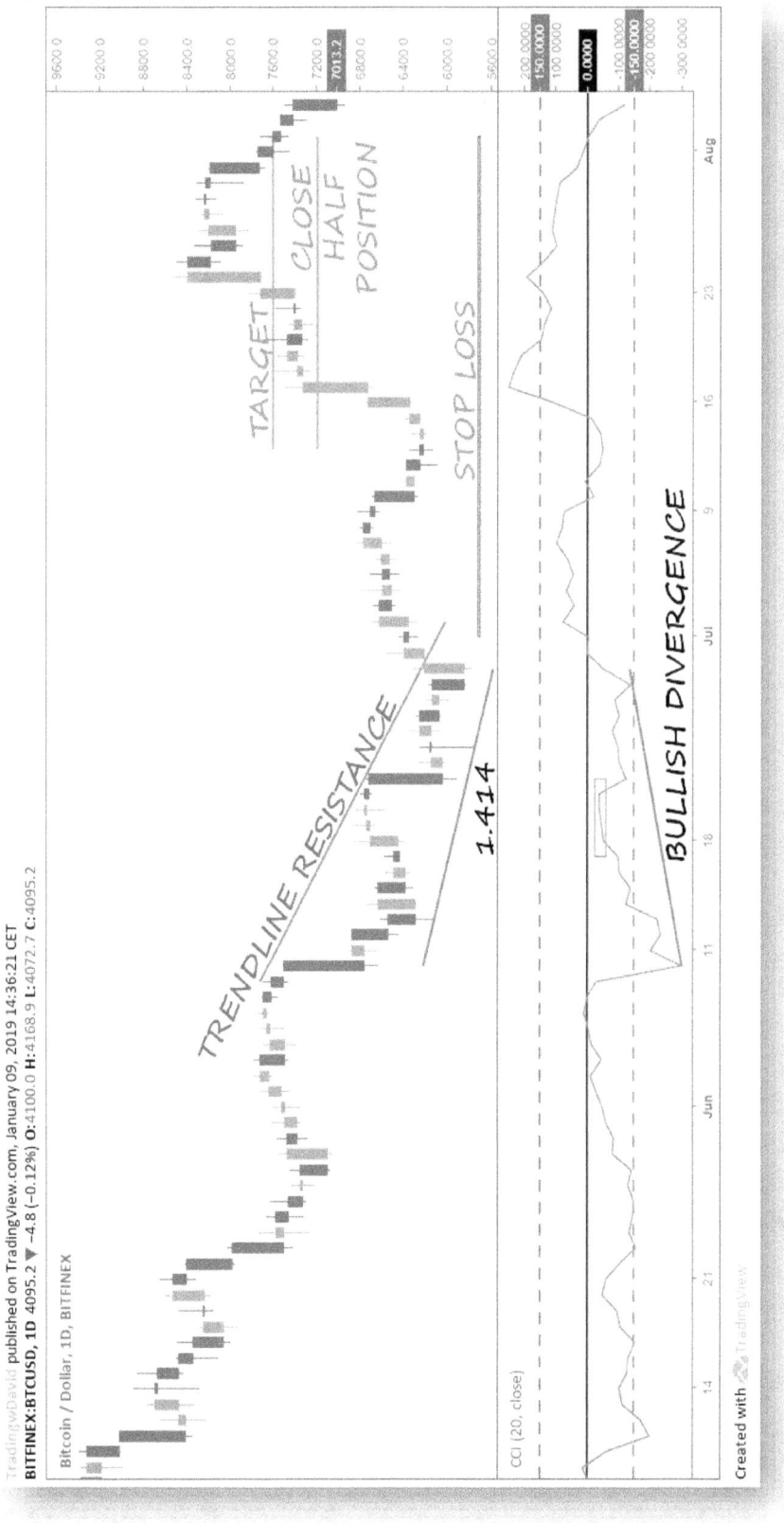

Figure 23 - BTC-Usd, bullish divergence (TradingView.com)

A bearish divergence on Aud-Jpy chart in figure 24.

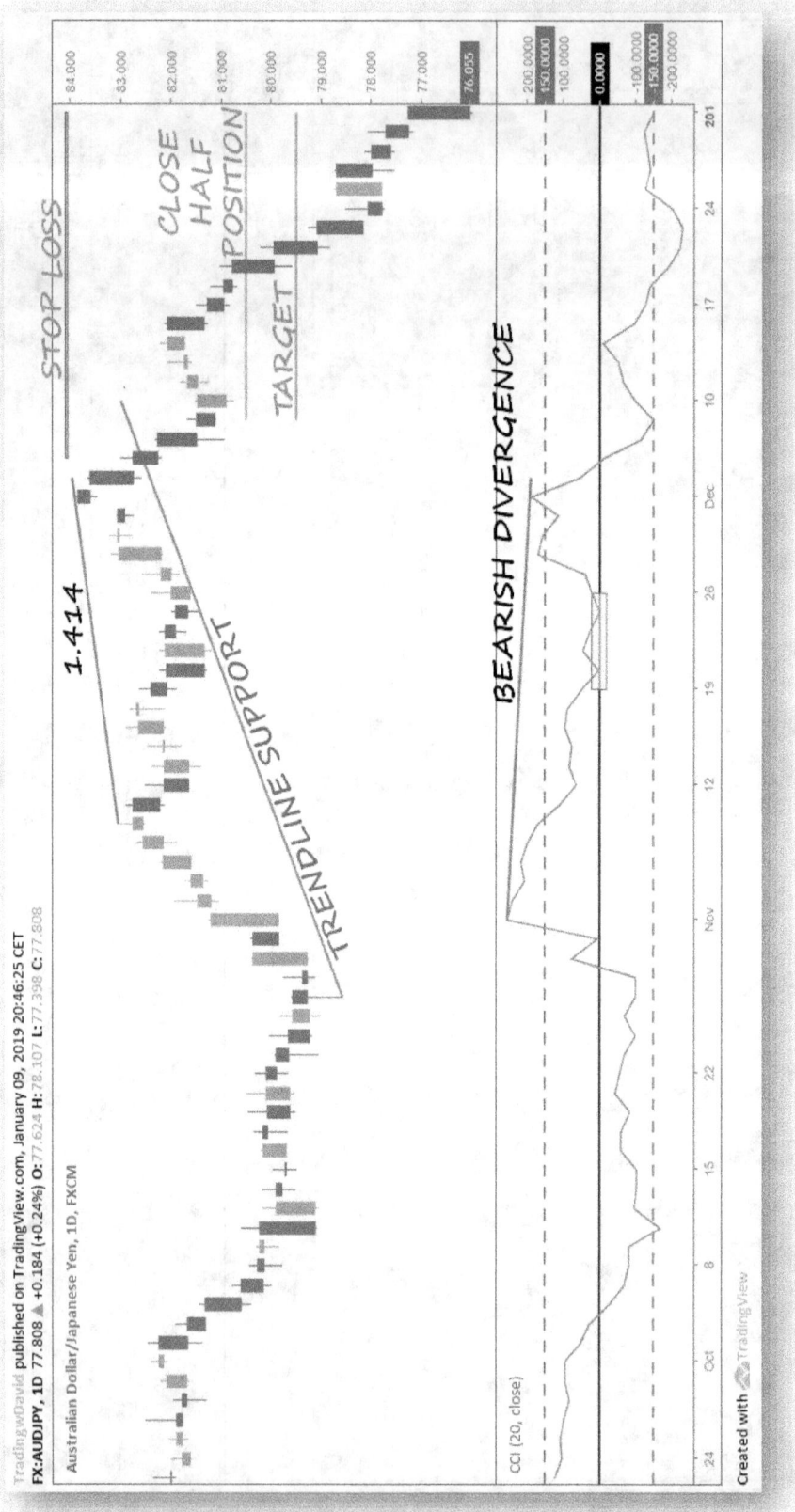

Figure 24 - Aud-Jpy, bearish divergence (TradingView.com)

A bullish divergence on Alibaba chart in figure 25.

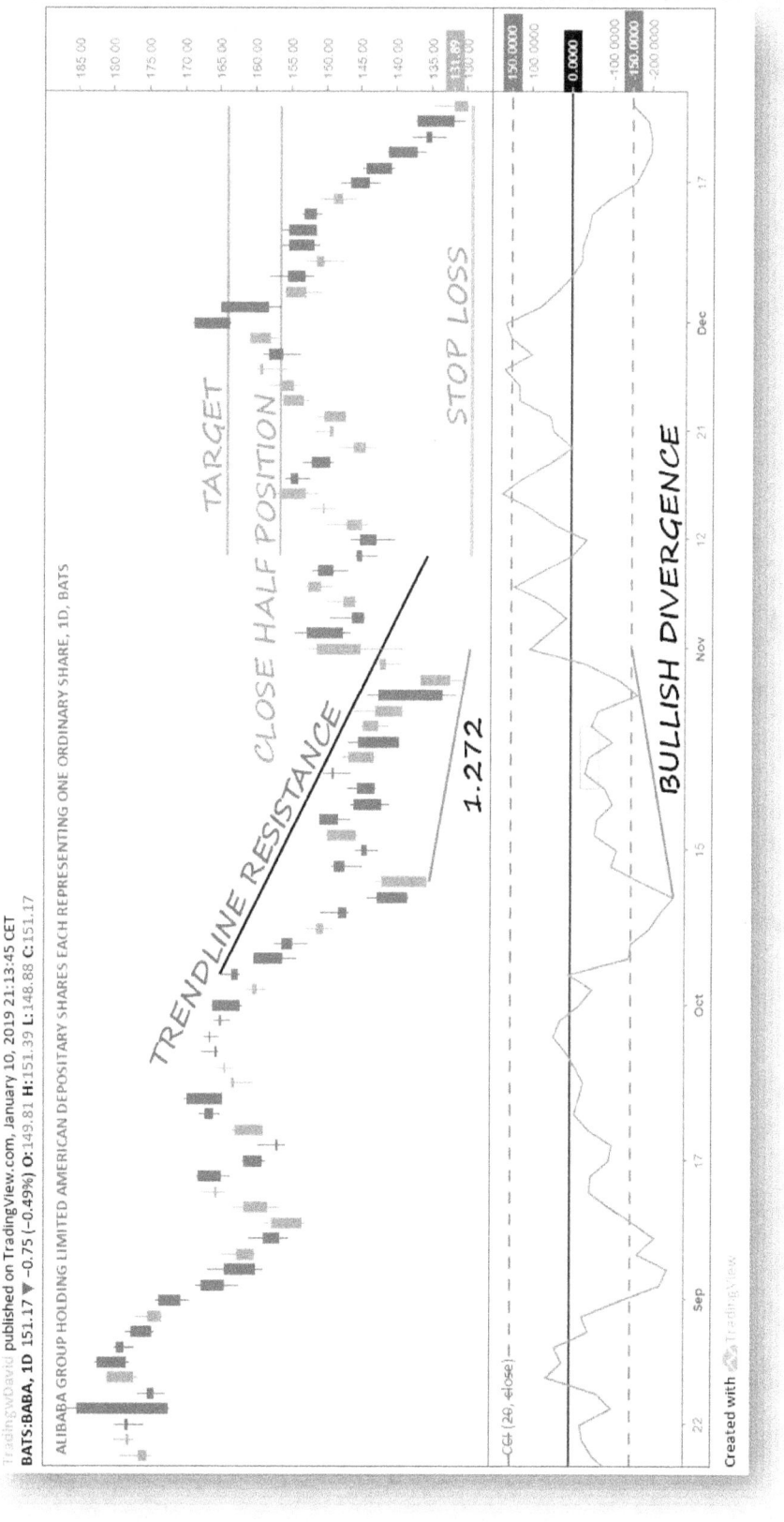

Figure 25 - Alibaba, bullish divergence (TradingView.com)

A bullish divergence on the LAM Research chart in figure 26.

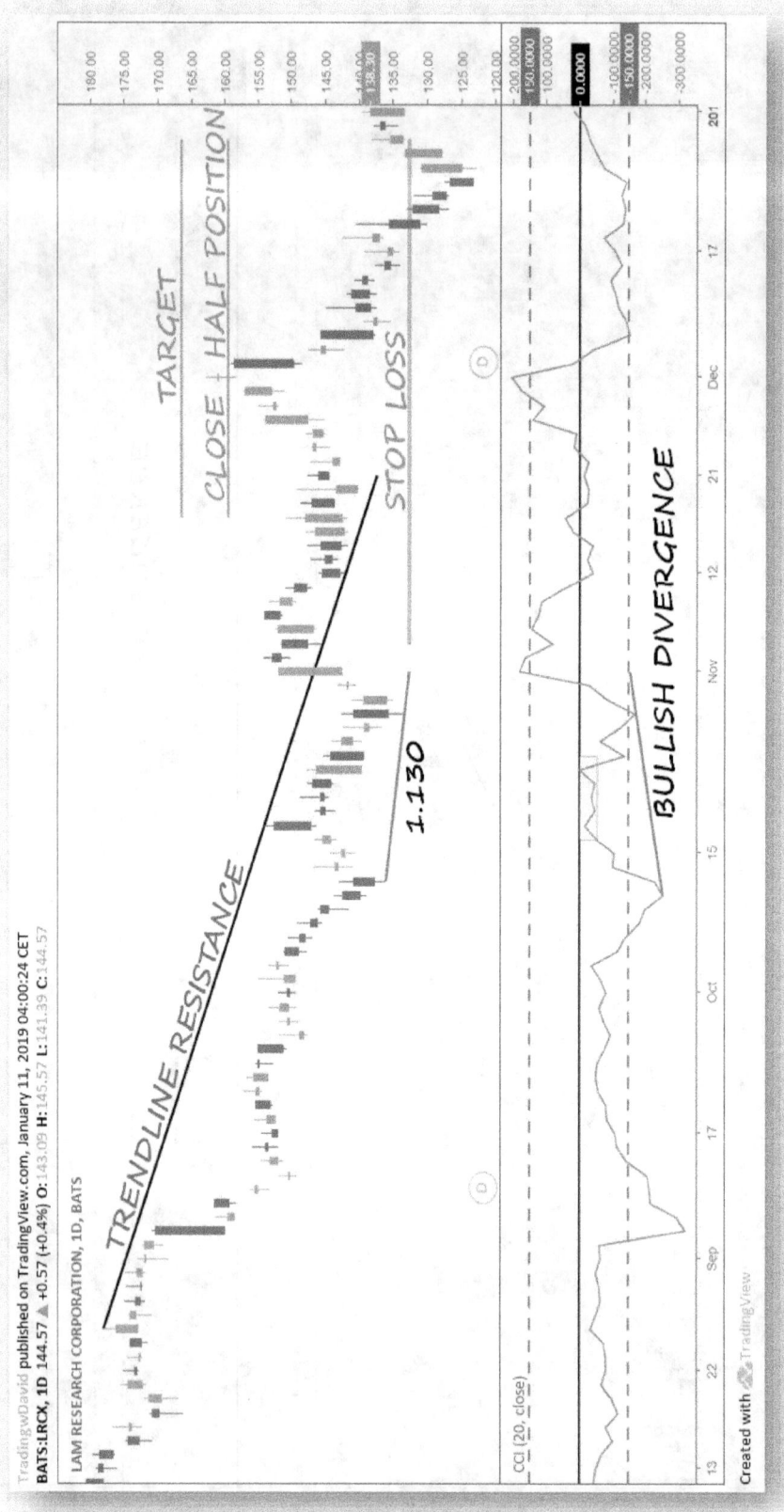

Figure 26 - LAM Research, bullish divergence (TradingView.com)

The target is the only aspect of this strategy that can be modified according to your kind of trading. You are free to decide where to take profit. What is essential is that the Risk/Reward is at least 1:1.

You can also decide to leave a part of the position open, by trying to ride larger movements. The method you saw applied in the examples above is the one that best suits my type of trading, as it gives me the best results.

As you can see in the last example, the price does not always hit my target. The market movement may stop first. With my system, I am sure to take home at least part of the "virtual" gain, and moving the stop at break-even means that I no longer risk anything.

I am going to conclude this chapter with a couple of clarifications. I did not talk about the Commodity Channel Index setting. I use it with a 20-period, but you can set it as you prefer, i.e., with the 14-period (usually the default setting) or another value. It is evident that a different period in the indicator can give different signals.

Another aspect is the time-frame. As I mentioned at the beginning of the chapter, a divergence often anticipates the inversion or slowing of a violent directional phase. The higher the time-frame, the greater the importance and the profundity of the movements that could follow.

I use this strategy mostly on daily time-frames. I rarely do on 4-hour time-frames, and never on lower ones. I also sometimes use the weekly time-frame; the signals are excellent even though it takes a long time to complete the trade.

What you have seen, therefore, is the strategy I use with divergences, a very simple and clear strategy. In the next chapter, I will show you how to open a correct position size, a fundamental aspect that most traders ignore.

MONEY MANAGEMENT

CHAPTER 3

It would be impossible to talk about money management in its entirety in just a couple of pages, so in this chapter I will be discussing position size in particular. In simple terms, it concerns what the correct position to open a trade is, based on the stop-loss you have decided and the maximum loss you are willing to suffer if the price reaches it.

As I specified at the beginning of the book, this strategy can be used in all the financial markets. There are different ways to calculate the position size, depending on the type of market. Below, I am going to go over the calculations for Shares, CFDs, and ETFs, and then, the one for Forex.

Stocks, CFDs, ETFs

Regardless of whether you operate with Stocks, CDFs or ETFs, the calculation is simple and always the same. Below is the formula:

Number of shares (LONG) = Max loss / (entry price – stop-loss)

Number of shares (SHORT) = Max loss / (stop-loss – entry price)

So, if for example you open a long position on Twitter with an entry price of $31.00, a stop-loss set at $28.00, and a maximum loss of $400, the number of shares to buy would be:

Number of shares (LONG) = Max loss / (entry price – stop-loss)

So:

Number of shares = $ 400 / ($ 31.00 – $ 28.00) = 133.34

According to your maximum loss and stop-loss, the number of shares you have to buy is 133. If the price reaches the stop-loss, you will lose $ 400.

If instead you establish the maximum loss not with a fixed amount of dollars (or in other currency) but with a percentage, the formula varies as follows:

Nr. of shares (LONG) = (capital x %of max loss) / (entry price – stop-loss)

Nr. of shares (SHORT) = (capital x %of max loss) / (stop-loss – entry price)

Where **capital** is the amount of money in your trading account and **%of max loss** is the maximum percentage of the money (in your account) you are willing to lose in the trade.

If for example you have an account of $ 60,000 and you decide to open a short position in Apple with entry price of $ 240.00 and stop-loss set at $ 245.00, with a maximum loss of 0.5% of the money in your account, the number of shares to sell is:

Nr. of shares (SHORT) = (capital x %of max loss) / (stop-loss – entry price)

So:

Number of shares = ($ 60,000 * 0.5%) / ($ 245.00 – $ 240.00) = 60

According to your percentage of maximum loss and your stop-loss, the number of shares you have to sell is 60. In this way, if the price hits the stop-loss, your loss will be exactly the amount you have established, $ 300 (which correspond to 0.5% of $ 60,000).

Let us now take a look at the formula for calculating the position size in Forex.

Forex

Now, I am going to show how to open a proper position in Forex according to your risk appetite. Doing this means that, even though the currency pair may reach the stop-loss, this will not create any problems for your account or cause you to stress unnecessarily.

Say, for instance, that after analysing the Gbp-Jpy daily chart, you decide to sell the currency pair with an entry level at 142.000, a stop-loss set at 143.500, and a target at 139.000. If your maximum bearable loss is $300, how much should you invest in this trade? You can obtain the position size to open this formula as follows:

Position Size = [(1,000 * max loss) / pips of stop] / value 1 pip

Where: **max loss** is your maximum bearable loss ($ 300); **pips of stop** is the distance in pips from the entry price to the stop-loss (150 in this example); the **value of 1 pip** is the minimum value of a pip for $ 1,000 of purchase/sale of the currency pair (in the example Gbp-Jpy).

For calculating the value of 1 pip of a currency pair, you can use the tool available on the Myfxbook website (https://www.myfxbook.com/forex-calculators/pip-calculator), where you simply have to select the currency in "Account Currency", 1,000 in "Trade Size" and followed by a click on "Calculate." In this way, in the table below, you will get the last column that will show you the minimum value of the pip to be used for each currency pair.

Returning to the example, the position size to open is as follows:

Position Size = [(1,000 * max loss) / pips of stop] / value 1 pip

So:

Position Size = [(1,000 * $ 300) / 150] / 0.09 = $ 22,222

The position to open is of $22,000 (rounded down, but you can also round it up if you prefer). This is a trade that, if the price hits the stop-loss, it will cause you to lose $300.

If here you establish the maximum loss (in dollars or any other currency) using a percentage rather than a fixed amount, the formula will vary, as follows:

Position Size = [(1,000 * (capital x %of max loss)) / pips of stop] / value 1 pip

And again, here **capital** means the amount of money in your trading account, and **%of max loss** refers to the maximum percentage of money in your account that you are willing to lose in the trade.

If for example you have an account of $ 50,000 and you decide to open a long position on Eur-Chf with entry price of 1.1720, stop-loss set at 1.1580, and a maximum loss of 0.75%, the position size to open would be:

Position Size = [(1,000 * (capital x %of max loss)) / pips of stop] / value 1 pip

So:

Position Size = [(1,000 * ($ 50,000 x 0.75%)) / 140] / 0.10 = $ 26,785

The position to open is of $26,750 (rounded down). A trade that, if price hits the stop-loss, will cause a loss of $375, that is, of 0.75$ of your account.

What you have seen in this chapter is only a part of your money management and trading plan. Remember that you always have to put yourself in the best conditions to trade.

Final Comments

CHAPTER 4

I have sought to use this book to teach you the correct way of using divergences in trading. Do not be tricked by the fact that this book is widely distributed at printing price. This strategy, if you use it correctly and with the appropriate money management for your account, will give you a high percentage of profitable trades.

Mere divergence, by itself, does not mean anything; it can also continue for weeks. It needs a confirmation in order to generate a signal. You get this confirmation from the breakout of the trendline support or resistance of the price. But this is not everything. Three fundamental rules establish which divergences are the best to trade in, the ones that will give you the highest odds of success.

I have also shown that I work with divergences between the price of an underlying asset and an indicator, the Commodity Channel Index (CCI). I use the CCI as the indicator because I have noticed, over the years, that it provides excellent quality signals.

This strategy works on all the time-frames, Although the greater the time-frame, the more accurate the signals will be. I apply it, apart from in a few rare exceptions, on daily charts.

As I said, this strategy generates a high percentage of trades closed in gain. But no strategy is perfect, trades that will go in the opposite direction of that dictated by the signal, albeit rarely, will always happen.

I want to show you a trade that I did with Amazon. Below in figure 27, you can see the daily chart. In this case, a couple of days after I bought the shares, Amazon came back down and hit the stop-loss.

This example aims to encourage you to respect always all the rules you have seen explained. The strategy is profitable only if you are disciplined in applying it. And furthermore, it gives me the opportunity, at the end of the book, to repeat a concept which I consider to be very important.

Figure 27 - Amazon, bullish divergence (TradingView.com)

What I have explained to you is a good strategy but, after all, it is just a graphical strategy, and data, just like news and rumours, can always spoil the party, pushing the market in the opposite direction to your trade. For this reason, it is always essential to insert the stop loss, as I have shown in the examples.

Therefore remember, in trading it is not enough to have a good strategy, what really makes the difference is how you manage the whole operation, especially those that go in the wrong direction (therefore the losses). For this reason, I always insert a chapter about Money management in my books, and in particular, the concept of Position Sizing.

If you open a position and you are stressed or nervous, ask yourself why. In at least 90% of cases, the reason for this is due to heavy losses when a market moves against your trade. Unfortunately, the ever-widening leverage applied by the brokers makes it possible to open large trades with little money, and this inevitably leads to losing all the money you have on the account where an appropriate money management has not been used.

Even though some advertisements emphasise the fact that with leverage you can trade using some pocket change, reality is very different. It takes money to trade: to increase an account from of $ 1,000 into $ 100,000 takes a lot of time. The more you increase the percentage of monthly earnings, the more you increase the risk; until you lose your one thousand dollars.

You have to protect your money, not trivially risk it with operations in "gambling-style." To get it, you had to work and struggle, it would be foolish to then throw it away by giving it to the markets. Earning money with trading is possible, but you need a method and a lot of discipline.

And here I stop otherwise I could spend hours writing about discipline, money management, behavioural finance, etc. I only wanted to underline this fundamental principle yet again.

This book has come to an end. This strategy gives me a lot of satisfaction, and I am sure that, if you use it correctly, it will be the same for you. I conclude by thanking from the bottom of my heart Caroline for her efforts in proofreading this book into English, she was very kind and professional. You can contact her through her email: carolinewinter4@hotmail.com.

For any questions my email is info@tradingwithdavid.com. On my website https://tradingwithdavid.com you can find articles, analysis, books, and much more. You find my other books on Amazon: **https://amazon.com/author/davidcarli**.

You can also follow me on:

- **Twitter**: https://twitter.com/tradingwdavid;
- **Instagram**: https://www.instagram.com/tradingwithdavidoriginal/, with operational ideas and discussions of economics and financial markets;
- **YouTube**: https://www.youtube.com/channel/UCHB18Qsl0fm-eBULQEMsVSA;
- **TradingView**: https://www.tradingview.com/u/TradingwDavid.

Do not go yet; one last thing to do.

If you enjoyed this book or found it useful, I would be very grateful if you would post a short review on Amazon. Your support does make a difference, and I read all the reviews personally so I can get your feedback and make this book even better.

Thanks in advance for your support! I really hope that what you have read will help you in your trading.

Happy Trading to you all!

WEB RESOURCES

APPENDIX A

Below, summarised, are all the resources you have seen in this book, as well as others.

WEBSITE	LINK
Free Platform	
TradingView	https://www.tradingview.com
Follow me	
Website	https://tradingwithdavid.com
Twitter	https://twitter.com/tradingwdavid
Instagram	https://www.instagram.com/tradingwithdavidoriginal
YouTube	https://www.youtube.com/channel/UCHB18Qsl0fm-eBULQEMsVSA
TradingView	https://www.tradingview.com/u/TradingwDavid
Tools	
Pip Calculator	https://www.myfxbook.com/forex-calculators/pip-calculator
Resources	
Economic Calendar	https://tradingwithdavid.com/economic-calendar

Table 1 - Web resources

www.ingramcontent.com/pod-product-compliance
Lightning Source LLC
Chambersburg PA
CBHW080446220526
45465CB00007B/2783